YOU'RE STILL NOT CRAZY

YOU'RE STILL NOT CRAZY

YOU MAY BE AN EMPATH DEALING WITH A NARCISSIST

CAROLYN BOOKER-PIERCE

J Merrill Publishing, Inc., Columbus 43207
www.JMerrill.pub

Copyright © 2021 J Merrill Publishing, Inc.
All rights reserved. No part of this publication may be reproduced, distributed, or transmitted in any form or by any means, including photocopying, recording, or other electronic or mechanical methods, without the prior written permission of the publisher, except in the case of brief quotations embodied in critical reviews and certain other noncommercial uses permitted by copyright law. For permission requests, contact J Merrill Publishing, Inc., 434 Hillpine Drive, Columbus, OH 43207
Published 2021

Library of Congress Control Number:
ISBN-13: 978-1-954414-23-5 (Paperback)
ISBN-13: 978-1-954414-22-8 (eBook)

Title: You're Still Not Crazy
Author: Carolyn Booker-Pierce

CONTENTS

Introduction	vii
1. What is an Empath?	1
2. Are You a Physical or Emotional Empath?	13
3. Am I Dealing with a Narcissist?	25
4. Watch the Company You Keep	35
5. Energy Vampires and their Victims	43
6. Did You Pick the Narcissist, or Did the Narcissist Pick You?	53
7. No Thanks, I Will Drive	63
8. Taking Care of Your Physical and Emotional Health	67
9. Protecting Yourself from Drama Queens and Kings	73
10. You're Not Crazy	79
References	85
About the Author	89
Also by Carolyn Booker-Pierce	91

INTRODUCTION

Do you ever feel like you take on or carry the stresses of others by being in a relationship with them, being around them, or being in a crowd?

You know you have a gift of compassion.

However, you sense that your gift can sometimes feel like a curse or taken for granted. Have you ever thought or felt like you keep picking the same type of toxic people in your relationships? You may have thought, at first, that you were making the right choices because the people who show up in your relationships appear to be nice, loving, and kind.

There is certainly nothing wrong with you choosing a person that seems to be nice, caring, and kind.

Who wouldn't share the likes of a charming person that makes you smile and feel great?

Initially, that is how you can feel in an initial relationship with a person with a narcissistic personality disorder.

They can make you feel on top of the world in the beginning. However, later you may come to discover those charming people you have allowed in your life are not so nice, loving, and kind after all. Yet, somehow, they keep showing up, and you keep inviting them in.

If you have ever wondered why you keep having encounters with the same type of people, there may be an explainable reason why.

You may not be aware, and I hope to help you understand that it is not totally your fault. It is probably your highly sensitive and compassionate personality drawing the same type of people. Therefore, it is your responsibility not to allow that to keep happening.

In this book on Empaths and the Narcissist, you may come to discover you are indeed an empath if you have not already figured it out.

Empaths are very empathic and compassionate people opposite the narcissist. However, because of the empath's sensitive and compassionate nature, you will find out the narcissistic personally likes to target the empathic personality.

You will also learn the games played by the narcissist with empathic type personalities. They put on great acts to lure their victims into a relationship.

They will tap into the empath's emotions to form a relationship. Narcissists are great at charming others. Once in the relationship with the narcissist, they will play all types of mind games to get what they want.

They are good at convincing empaths that they said one thing and meant another. They will make a promise and not keep it. They will also lie about the promise they made.

The empath may begin to feel like they are going crazy, convinced something is wrong with them after being convinced of something that may or may not have happened.

In reality, because of the empath's compassionate heart, they are easily sucked in emotionally by the narcissist's manipulation and games. Good judgment and normalcy will fade into the narcissist's trap because they are good at conning others.

The compassionate and giving empath needs to learn how to take care of themselves so they are not easily overtaken by false appearance and cons of the narcissist.

Empaths usually fall into giving more than they take, unlike the narcissist, since they are traditionally givers by nature. However, after days, months, and years, giving their time, money, birthdays, holidays, and other special occasions is not reciprocated.

The empath will become stressed, sensing something they need to do to escape or is seriously wrong them. It is something wrong, but it can be corrected with some boundaries and discipline. Not knowing who they are or who they were created to be can leave the empath feeling insecure and inadequate.

There is nothing wrong with being an empath. The problem is not knowing you have a gift and when to use or not to use it.

Because empaths are highly empathic, compassionate, and giving people, they tend to attract the narcissist. But, on the other hand, because narcissists are self-centered and self-absorbed, it is easy for them always to present a sad story or a problem to get what they want.

That is important information for an empath to know to protect their gift. When you are a highly sensitive and compassionate person, it is easy to be taken advantage of by the narcissistic personality.

Empaths are highly sensitive to other needs and take on others' pain. It is easy for others to misuse the blessing of empath's compassion and empathy.

If a person has no emotional empathy like the narcissist, it is easy not to value another's compassion and sensitivity. That is why empaths are prime targets to the non-empathic, non-compassionate, and genuinely self-absorbed narcissist.

As an empath, you may do all the giving while the narcissist is doing all the taking. But, on the other hand, you may be so compassionate that you don't know how not to be unconcerned about others and their feelings.

After giving out so much of oneself, the empath can feel drained and confused about what is happening with them. As a result, they will begin to second guess themselves and their God-given personality.

While on the other hand, the narcissist, with their manipulation and lies, will try to convince the empath what they see taking place is not happening. Thus, causing the empath to think they are crazy.

You are not crazy. You're probably just a sensitive and compassionate empath dealing with a narcissist.

As you read this book, I hope the content will help you determine if you are an overly sensitive and compassionate empath targeted by a self-absorbed narcissist.

I also hope you learn how to take better care of yourself as an empath.

Understanding who you are as an empath and setting healthy boundaries will be vital as part of your survival. The more you know and understand about your gift, the greater your chance of embracing who you are as an empath.

No longer will you be the target for the narcissist. No longer will you be in the dark about the gift you have been given.

1

WHAT IS AN EMPATH?

I want to help you determine if you are an empath. However, you must first understand what an empath is?

There is a difference between one who commonly shows empathy versus an empath who connects to others and their pain on a higher emotional level.

An empathic personality is not your typical person with common empathy and compassion for another —in general, putting themselves in another's shoes.

In comparison, most of the common traits of empathy are found in an empath. Empath's sensitivity to others emotionally and physically is on a whole different level than one who shows common empathy. Merriam-Webster describes empathy as,

The action of understanding, being aware of, being sensitive to, and vicariously experiencing the feelings, thoughts, and experience of another of either the past or present without having the feelings, thoughts, and experience fully communicated in an objectively explicit manner.

Simply put, empathy is the ability to put our self in another's shoes without absorbing them emotionally. This may include understanding and feeling what others are feeling and being sensitive to what another is experiencing at the time or in the past, without emotions. Empaths tend to experience more emotions when it comes to their empathy for others. Merriam-Webster's definition of an empath is,

One who experiences the emotions of others : a person who has empathy for others.

In a Psychology Today article "10 traits Empathic People Share and how to look out for yourself if you are one," written by Judith Orloff MD she says,

The trademark of an empath is feeling and absorbing other people's emotions and, or, physical symptoms because of their high sensitivities. These people filter the world through their intuition and have a difficult time intellectualizing their feelings.

The word empath sounded like a label attached to a crazy person when I first heard about empaths. I should have known it was attached to the word empathy.

My heart is big on empathy. I knew my empathy and compassion for caring about others' pain and hurting people was greater than most common people. I used to think something was wrong with me for caring so much for those down on the luck, so to speak.

My children still to this day give me funny looks when I bring someone new into my home that may not have a place to stay. So, I have invited the homeless, the hungry, the person struggling with substance abuse, the person that just needed a temporary place to stay, that homeless person, or the one who had nowhere to go.

Sometimes it would be the person that most people don't want to be bothered with. So, I tell myself this is the last time I will do this. Still, my compassionate and emotional heart will not always let me say no due to their circumstances. That is empathic behavior.

Empaths hurt when others hurt. Empaths can feel the pain of homelessness when someone is homeless. Empaths can feel the pain of others' rejection.

However, common sense does kick in most of the time in some dangerous situations that might compromise my safety and the well-being of my family. I don't believe I have had any serial killers, cult members, or initially noticeable crazy person living with me yet. That is outwardly apparent crazy people. I am sure my children would beg to differ with that statement.

I have friends who have called me a softy. I can be soft until you cross me. While it takes a lot for me to notice I have been taken advantage of, I will eventually come to my senses.

When I feel that I have been crossed or taken advantage of, the wisdom of protection emerges, saying, "time to cut this person off with the gift of goodbye." When I have had to use the gift of "goodbye," I seem totally opposite of my empathic personality. That gift is only used when forced or necessary.

Remember, it takes a lot for me to use that precious gift. However, the gift of goodbye has saved me from being used more than I would have been taken advantage of because of my guilt over having to say no.

Because of the empath's naturally affectionate personality and high sensitivity to other people's emotions, they can easily become a target for the narcissist.

What is a Narcissist? I am glad you asked. According to Merriam Webster definition of a narcissist is the following,

an individual showing symptoms of or suffering from narcissism: such as. a : an extremely self-centered person who has an exaggerated sense of self-importance. b : a person who is overly concerned with his or her physical appearance.

Simply put, narcissists are extremely self-centered and self-absorbed. It is all about them and their agenda. They can be so concerned about their own stuff that they will lie and manipulate to meet their needs.

Narcissists tend to have an eye for people who care deeply and are sensitive to others in need, such as empaths. Therefore, the narcissist will always present with a need once he gets in good with an empath. Especially when it comes to those they are in a relationship with, like family, friends, and spouses. I should know. I am an empath.

Because of my sensitive and compassionate heart, I have been conned and lured into many unhealthy relationships with narcissists. So, it has been with friendships, dating relationships, and even marriage to the narcissist. I am a giver and a good listener by nature. I'm a social worker and a counselor. Go figure.

You will find plenty of empaths in the field of social work, counseling, nursing, doctors, and anything concerning meeting the needs of others. Empaths are usually willing to listen to the narcissist's sad stories about being down on their luck, sick, depressed, and homeless. Empathy will quickly kick in where there seems to be a serious problem that needs to be fixed.

Empaths will listen when the narcissist comes with a need they can't meet and how nobody cares about them. A story as to why it was someone else's fault their relationship ended badly.

Narcissists never tell the whole story. They tell part of the truth, enough to get the empath's attention and emotionally involved in the story. Once the narcissist knows they have the empath emotionally, the empath becomes chopped liver to their scheme. Dr. Judith Orloff shares this number 1 of the 10 traits she writes on an empath,

Empaths are naturally giving, spiritually open, and good listeners. If you want heart, empaths have got it. Through thick and thin, these world-class nurturers will be there for you. But they can easily have their feelings hurt, too: Empaths are often told that they are "too sensitive" and need to "toughen up."

Empaths compassionate giving can be a blessing and a curse. Their giving is a blessing to those really in need and not trying to take advantage of their giving. However, their giving becomes a curse when they fall into the hands of a natural-born narcissist who lives to see who they can con and take advantage of next.

The narcissistic personality manipulates for their own satisfaction and good. They are good at what they do. They will prey on those who are as compassionate, giving, and sensitive as I can be. They are not capable of feeling emotions. They are capable of manipulating and conning compassionate people for their own selfish needs.

They start very charming and full of promises. They are so good at charming others they begin to believe their own lies. Now can you see how a narcissist can get into the heart of an empath and those around them?

Narcissists can spot an empath a mile away because of the way they give attention to those around them. A narcissist can see that empaths are loyal and stick by you through thick and thin and a lot of time through their negative, misleading, and addictive behaviors. Even after the narcissist has hurt an empath's feelings, most empaths believe in giving second chances, forgiving, and more.

The empath will continue to give to the narcissist compassion until they become so filled with stress and drama it becomes a me or them situation. If the empath is not strong or healthy, it becomes the empath, not them. The narcissist will suck the life out of an empathic personality. That is why they are labeled as vampires. I will talk about that later.

I will say empaths should take care in how they absorb other people's pain and problems. Judith Orloff, in her book, The Empath's Survival Guides, Life Strategies for Sensitive People, says,

Empaths are emotional sponges, who absorb both the stress and joy of the world, we feel everything.

You can tell an empath that you don't have food, and the empath will give you theirs. They can emotionally feel your need to be fed. You can say your electric was turned off, and the empath will worry about your electric and either pay your bill or be sick over the fact you and your children are in the dark. Sicker if they can't pay the bill for you.

Empaths can become physically sick and share your symptoms. For example, if you share you are experiencing extreme pain and share the symptoms with an empath, they will begin to take on the same feelings of despair. Or an empath may be listening to a close friend share how they have become overwhelmed and depressed with life. If the empath listens long enough, the empath will start to become overwhelmed and depressed.

Some empaths have been accused of being hypochondriacs as a result of taking on others' sickness and pain. That is called a physical empath. You know that person that every symptom you tell them you have like a backache, headache, muscle ache? They have the same physical problem. Because they could be an empath, not all empaths will grab their back and say, "Yes, my back hurts all the time too." Their head and muscle may start to hurt.

If you are emotionally upset, the empath can take on your emotions and quickly become emotionally upset. I can watch a movie and cry like a baby with the person in the film if they are hurting or emotionally upset. Don't let the person die or lose a loved one. I cry harder than the actors enough to win an academy award.

I am highly sensitive and emotional. I just don't always let people in public see it. I work at a jail for crying out loud. I know how to be tough. However, I can still show compassion when appropriate and take on another's feelings of emotion. I came home the other day and turned on Dr. Phil. Big mistake. I sat down to relax and what they had on was a painful story about a mother whose best friend was asked to babysit her toddler.

Later that night, she got a call from the police asking her to come to the hospital. Her best friend had killed her baby for no reported reason. I was in tears absorbing that mother's pain. As a sensitive empath, it is important to be careful of the type of television shows that are watched, as well as movies. The news can be another emotional trigger for the empath. It is possible to watch the wrong thing and end up in a corner somewhere looking crazy after absorbing the character's energy, negative press, or someone's crisis. I have found myself like that many times.

I am an empath. What about you? In the next chapter, I will share with you more information regarding emotional and physical empaths.

2

ARE YOU A PHYSICAL OR EMOTIONAL EMPATH?

As you know from my earlier confession, I am an emotional empath. I am still on the fence when it comes to owning being a physical empath. I am very sensitive to others' emotional anxiety, emotional pain, and frustrations. I can usually sense when someone is hurting or having a hard time. When a person decides to share their pain or why they are hurting, then I tend to absorb every detail no matter how hard I try not to allow myself to become highly emotional over their problem. Then I attempt to fix whatever is causing the person pain or fix what is broken. If a person is stressed, I want to fix whatever is stressing the person to the point I can become stressed.

Caring about other people and their needs is what I sometimes do until I make myself sick. I am not as bad as I used to be because I have learned to take better care of myself - especially after being worn out with several narcissists that drained the life out of me. Go figure. I am an empathic fixer, and narcissists are self-absorbed users of sensitive people like me. Mix the two, and you have a real recipe for disaster.

Emotional empaths and physical empaths are the two types of empaths I am most familiar with. That is why emotional and physical empaths are the only two types of empaths I will discuss in this book. I am not by no means an expert on either topic. I am just sharing my two cents on what I have personally experienced, read, and learned about being an empath. To help you determine if you are a physical empath or emotional empath, I will refer to Judith Orloff's, The Empaths Survival Guide, Physical and Emotional Empath Self-Assessment section of her book (p34-35),

Am I A PHYSICAL EMPATH?

Ask yourself the following questions:

- Have I ever sat next to someone in pain and started to feel pain too?

- Do I get physically ill in crowds?
- Have I been called a hypochondriac but know my symptoms are real?
- Do I react to other people's stress by developing a physical symptom in my own body?
- Do I get energized by some people and depleted by others?
- Do I frequently go to doctors without getting treatment that helps?
- Am I chronically fatigued, or do I have mysterious and unexplained ailments?
- Do I often feel exhausted by crowds, preferring to stay home?
- Is my body sensitive to sugar, alcohol, and processed foods?

Am I AN EMOTIONAL EMPATH?

Ask yourself the following questions:

- Do I pick up other people's emotions, such as anxiety, anger, or frustrations?
- Do I get an emotional hangover after an argument or a conflict?
- Do I feel depressed or anxious in crowds?
- Do I want to fix people and take away their stress?
- Can I intuit other people's feelings, even when they are unexpressed? Is it hard to distinguish other people's emotions from my own?
- Do I care so much about others that I neglect my own needs?
- Do I overeat to cope with difficult people or emotional stress?
- Do I experience mood swings from sugar, carbohydrates, other specific foods?

Orloff says,

> Here's how to interpret the self-assessment:

- One to two yeses in a category indicate that you're partially that type of empath.

- Three to four yeses indicate that you are moderately that type of empath.

- Five or more yeses indicate that you're definitely that type of empath.

Identifying if you are a physical or emotional empath is important in helping you understand more about yourself and how to cope when in certain situations. For example, it can help you understand that you are not crazy the way you may sometimes feel. Or how people like a narcissist can sometimes make you feel when dealing with him or her in a relationship.

While I still have a lot to learn and figure out about myself as an empath. I do think it is important to share what information I do know. For a long time, I did not have a name for what type of personality I had, being a highly sensitive and compassionate person. Now I can name what I am experiencing and who I am as an empath. Now I am taking better care of myself and my emotions. In this book, I am mainly referring to the physical and emotional empaths. Judith Orloff's says this about the physical and emotional empaths,

> Physical Empaths. You are especially attuned to other people's physical symptoms and tend to absorb them into your body. You also can become energized by someone's sense of well-being.

I hope you are starting to see what can happen when a physical empath is around others who have or suffer physical pain. Physical empaths will absorb that pain, especially if they are around someone sickly or complaining about their pain. On the other hand, take someone who has healthy positive energy or the opposite energy. The emotional empath can easily be attuned to that person's high or low energy emotionally.

Emotional Empaths. You mainly pick up other people's emotions and can become a sponge for their feelings, both happy and sad.

You can't always choose who you will be around, especially your job, community settings, and family members. It is, however, important to be aware of your own sensitivities and personality as an empath. Remember, if you are an empath, you can and will absorb others' energy. Narcissistic-type personalities will target you because of your sensitivities and compassion just to manipulate you. They are self-absorbed, looking for people they can con or take advantage of. The narcissist will see the empath's compassion as a sign of weakness and an opportunity to get what they want and to meet their own selfish needs.

Being an empath is not a bad thing it is a gift. It is a gift that can be misunderstood and misused by others. It is a gift that should be embraced and nurtured. In the times we are currently living in, the world needs more empathy and empathic type people. The world does not need more narcissistic-type people using and abusing them. That kind of person only cares about and is a lover of themselves. The scripture refers to them as narcissistic and self-focused people in the last days. Unfortunately, we are living in the last days. 2 Timothy 3:1-3 (AMP) exhorts us,

> *But understand this, that in the last days dangerous times [of great stress and trouble] will come [difficult days that will be hard to bear]. 2 For people will be lovers of self [narcissistic, self-focused], lovers of money [impelled by greed], boastful, arrogant, revilers, disobedient to*

parents, ungrateful, unholy and profane.

Yes, this is the world we currently live in. The good thing is there are still empathic-type people in the world. However, they need to be aware that there are narcissistic-type people in the world too. The lovers of self, self-focused, lovers of money, boastful, arrogant, lacking compassion and empathy.

Because the times we live in are dangerous, full of stress and emotional vampires, physical and emotional empaths must be careful not to take on other people's physical pain and emotional pain. If they are not careful to take care of themselves by setting healthy boundaries, physical and emotional empaths can become depleted by others.

Suppose a person finds themselves frequently going to the doctor without getting treatment for the symptoms. In that case, that could be a sure sign they are absorbing other people's pain and or sickness. Likewise, being chronically fatigued can be something a physical or emotional empath can experience after being exhausted by other's pain and by crowds like parties, big events, and things involving a lot of energy from many people.

I am a social worker and an emotional empath. That means I like to help and fix other people's problems. That also means I work with people with problems for a living.

If I am not careful to control my emotions, I can absorb a lot of people's emotions, such as anxiety, anger, or frustrations. Depending on how many people I interact with, having those emotions I just mentioned can determine how tired I may be at the end of a working day.

I have experience going home with an emotional hangover from just listening to how others dealt with physical abuse, drug abuse, and fear of going to prison. They have custody battles with Child Protective Services, the other child's parent, and foster care services. I listen to how they fight through their day with estranged family members, corrections officers, and those in their dorm.

Did I mention I work at a county jail?

I listen to others' problems because that is what I do. I am a fixer by nature and by profession. With that comes a desire to take away other people's pain and stress.

When I go home, I sometimes do the same because people know that I will listen. Therefore, I am subject to go home and take in more of other people's problems. While I am a lot better at drawing a line with boundaries, there was a time I stayed tired because I did not know how to stop helping.

I know how to now because I am getting older and wiser. I have learned to set better boundaries and take better care of myself.

When you are a physical or emotional empath, setting boundaries for yourself and others will be essential to your survival. Knowing and understanding your own feeling versus feelings that belongs to someone else will be important as well. For example, if you feel sad, but nothing in life is going on that would cause you to be sad, you may need to examine your last conversations. That may help you figure out where you may have picked up the sad emotions. But, again, they may be from someone else.

Suppose you feel drained every time you are around a certain type of personality, like the narcissist. In that case, that may be a sign you are taking on someone else's stuff other than your own. Narcissistic personalities can easily unload their problems with their manipulation and charm that can cause a person to turn away from their own needs to focus on theirs. They don't have a problem dumping on someone else. They are self-centered.

When you're neglecting yourself because you give more of your time, money, and emotions to someone else, you may be an empath dealing with a narcissistic personality. But, first, you must ask yourself, "Am I dealing with a narcissist?"

3

AM I DEALING WITH A NARCISSIST?

It is important to know as an empath if you are dealing with is a narcissistic personality. Narcissists can be very toxic to an empath in a relationship because of the empath's highly sensitive and compassionate vulnerabilities. Empaths can be easily manipulated and taken advantage of because they want to help and fix others. Narcissists are the opposite. They want all the help they can get and are not very caring about others' needs.

- Ask yourself if they are taking more than they are giving.
- Ask yourself if the conversations are

consistently all about the other person you are communicating with.
- Ask yourself if you feel drained every time you interact with someone you suspect could be a narcissist.

The questions are necessary if you plan on being in any type of relationship with a narcissist or need to avoid the narcissist altogether. It is extremely important to know if the person is a narcissist if you are an empath. The empath's sensitive and compassionate nature is easily targeted and manipulated by narcissistic people or those with a narcissistic personality disorder. I have included the following information for your further assessment of a potential narcissist by Preston Ni's Article from Psychology Today, Posted on 9/14/2014, the 10 Signs That You're in a Relationship with a Narcissist,

> 1. Conversation Hoarder. The narcissist loves to talk about him or herself, and doesn't give you a chance to take part in a two-way conversation. You struggle to have your views and feelings heard. When you do get a word in, if it's not in agreement with the narcissist, your comments are

likely to be corrected, dismissed, or ignored.

"My father's favorite responses to my views were: 'but...,' 'actually...,' and 'there's more to it than this...' He always has to feel like he knows better."

— Anonymous

2. Conversation Interrupter. While many people have the poor communication habit of interrupting others, the narcissist interrupts and quickly switches the focus back to herself. He shows little genuine interest in you.

3. Rule Breaker. The narcissist enjoys getting away with violating rules and social norms, such as cutting in line, chronic under-tipping (some will overtip to show off), stealing office supplies, breaking multiple appointments, or disobeying traffic laws.

"I take pride in persuading people to give me exceptions to their rules"

— Anonymous

4. Boundary Violator. Shows wanton disregard for other people's thoughts, feelings, possessions, and physical space. Oversteps and uses others without consideration or sensitivity. Borrows items or money without returning. Breaks promises and obligations repeatedly. Shows little remorse and blames the victim for one's own lack of respect.

"It's your fault that I forgot because you didn't remind me"

— Anonymous

5. False Image Projection. Many narcissists like to do things to impress others by making themselves look good externally. This "trophy" complex can exhibit itself physically, romantically, sexually, socially, religiously, financially, materially, professionally, academically, or culturally. In these situations, the narcissist uses people, objects, status, and/or accomplishments to represent the self, substituting for the perceived, inadequate "real" self. These

grandstanding "merit badges" are often exaggerated. The underlying message of this type of display is: "I'm better than you!" or "Look at how special I am—I'm worthy of everyone's love, admiration, and acceptance!"

"I dyed my hair blond and enlarged my breasts to get men's attention—and to make other women jealous."

— Anonymous

"My accomplishments are everything."

— Anonymous executive

"I never want to be looked upon as poor. My fiancé and I each drive a Mercedes. The best man at our upcoming wedding also drives a Mercedes."

— Anonymous

In a big way, these external symbols become pivotal parts of the narcissist's false identity, replacing the real and injured self.

6. Entitlement. Narcissists often expect preferential treatment from others.

They expect others to cater (often instantly) to their needs, without being considerate in return. In their mindset, the world revolves around them.

7. Charmer. Narcissists can be very charismatic and persuasive. They make you feel very special and wanted when they're interested in you (for their own gratification). However, once they lose interest in you (most likely after they've gotten what they want or became bored), they may drop you without a second thought. On the other hand, a narcissist can be very engaging and sociable, as long as you're fulfilling what she desires and giving her all of your attention.

8. Grandiose Personality. Thinking of oneself as a hero or heroine, a prince or princess, or one of a kind special person. Some narcissists have an exaggerated sense of self-importance, believing that others cannot live or survive without his or her magnificent contributions.

"I'm looking for a man who will treat my daughter and me like princesses"

— Anonymous singles ad

"Once again I saved the day—without me, they're nothing"— Anonymous

9. Negative Emotions. Many narcissists enjoy spreading and arousing negative emotions to gain attention, feel powerful, and keep you insecure and off-balance. They are easily upset at any real or perceived slights or inattentiveness. They may throw a tantrum if you disagree with their views, or fail to meet their expectations. They are extremely sensitive to criticism, and typically respond with heated argument (fight) or cold detachment (flight). On the other hand, narcissists are often quick to judge, criticize, ridicule, and blame you. Some narcissists are emotionally abusive. By making you feel inferior, they boost their fragile ego, and feel better about themselves.

"Some people try to be tall by cutting off the heads of others."

— Paramhansa Yogananda

10. Manipulation: Using Others as an Extension of Self. Making decisions for others to suit one's own needs. The narcissist may use his or her romantic partner, child, friend, or colleague to meet unreasonable self-serving needs, fulfill unrealized dreams, or cover up self-perceived inadequacies and flaws.

"If my son doesn't grow up to be a professional baseball player, I'll disown him"

— Anonymous father

"Aren't you beautiful? Aren't you beautiful? You're going to be just as pretty as mommy"

— Anonymous mother

Manipulation and conning others are like a natural trait for the narcissist. Narcissists are good at their charm and telling others what they want to hear. If you get caught up in the charm of the narcissist you will miss the fact you have been set up for what is next to come. That is usually something he or she wants from you or wants you to do.

Ni also writes this about the manipulation of the narcissist,

> Another way narcissists manipulate is through guilt, such as proclaiming, "I've given you so much, and you're so ungrateful," or, "I'm a victim—you must help me or you're not a good person." They hijack your emotions, and beguile you to make unreasonable sacrifices.

Empaths, because they can be highly emotional, should beware if a narcissist gives them something, especially something of value. They will expect you to give back twice as much in return or guilt you if you don't. Remember, it is all about them and meeting their physical and emotional needs.

4

WATCH THE COMPANY YOU KEEP

Have you ever heard the saying, "You are the company you keep"?

That does not have to be a bad thing. I try to be around positive influential people. I like being encouraged. I am an encourager.

I have learned that being around good positive energy is healthy for me as an empath. Positive energy helps me to grow, while negative energy does the opposite. I love to have good thought challenging conversations. I also love to laugh.

In the times we live in right now with all the political stuff, police-involved shootings, and the Coronavirus, there is not much to laugh about these days. It is important to be intentional about creating positive attitudes and energy to thrive in a hostile world. Therefore, if you are going to have company, why not make it good company.

If you are going to be around trouble, why not be around good trouble, trouble that fights for what is right and good. Hang out with positive people - people who know how to be in a crisis and not be the crisis. I know a lot of people. However, I know I can't afford to be around and talk to certain people all the time.

Honestly, some people I know will drain me if I give them too much of my time and energy. Whether you are an empath or not, you probably know people that are draining.

There are a few people I can spend hours talking with because of their positive energy. I apologize to one of my sisters all the time. She lives out of state, so it is like taking in a breath of fresh air when I talk to her.

She allows me to release some of the things I have taken on emotionally that drains me. She usually refuels me in a healthy way. I usually talk to her for at least an hour or more. I don't do it on purpose. It is just easy to talk with her.

My sister is not a drainer, and she is not selfish. On the contrary, she is sweet and possibly an empath full of compassion like me.

I am close with all my sisters. We can talk, laugh, and be ourselves with no judgment. The one sister I am speaking of lives so far away I don't get to see her as much. Therefore, I talk to her longer than my other siblings.

My children are mature adults. I don't see them every day. However, when I do see them, I can hang out with them for hours.

I have a few good spiritual friends I can talk to and hang out with who also have positive energy. Notice is said a few good friends. That is all I need.

All those I just mentioned encourage me, challenge me, and most pray for me. I generally feel good and not exhausted after being around or talking to those I just mentioned. However, imagine being around someone who is depressed, sick, or needy all the time.

As an empath, remember we tend to absorb both the physical and emotions of others. Therefore, which would you rather choose to keep company with? The positive energy influencing company you keep or energy vampires that will drain the life out of you?

It is draining to think about those types of people who need something all the time—those who complain and never have a good day. You know who they are in your life. You get the feeling of dread when you see them on your caller ID, run into them in public, or work with them on your job. They are the ones you know not to ask how they are doing. They are the ones who are never happy and can't wait to tell you their latest bad news. You are not trying to be mean when you try to get away. You are trying to stay healthy.

Do I spend hours talking to those types of people? No, not if I can avoid it.

That is a recipe to bring me down in my emotions and spirit. Some people in the world enjoy being depressed and bringing others down with them. They don't feel right when they are feeling normal. They only feel right when they are emotionally hurting or in pain. Then there are your hypochondriacs in the world as well. According to Merriam Webster's definition of a hypochondriac, a person who is often or always worried about his or her own health: a person affected.

Those are usually the ones who will grab their back when you tell them you have backache. If your head is hurting, theirs is hurting too. However, suppose something like the Coronavirus is the latest epidemic. In that case, they will have every symptom and be the first ones in the doctor's office.

They worry about their health constantly. Physical empaths have sometimes been confused with and accused of being hypochondriacs. However, some do experience the same symptoms as those around them who are sick and or depressed.

Thank God I don't experience others' sickness or depression. I do well on my own with enough of that given my age and the pandemic getting on my nerves.

Some just are angry most of the time. Just mad at the world and for being in it. That person will always show up ready to tell you how bad things are and who their victim of the day is that they are mad at. Usually, someone does not even know they were picked as the "I am mad at you" person of the day.

You can be in the best of moods, then here comes Angry Andy or Depressed Debbie. I am sorry if your name happens to be one or the other. It was not directed at you. People will start to scatter when that type of energy shows up in a room. But guess what the empath will do most of the time? You guessed it. Most empaths will stick around feeling sorry for the angry or depressed person because empaths are highly sensitive when it comes to hurting another's feelings.

Unlike the self-absorbed narcissist who will not stick around if it is not about him or her. Empaths will stay and soak up all the angry and depressed energy if they are not careful. Then they will leave with all that negative energy because they have been in the company of an angry or depressed person.

If the angry person is mad with their spouse, beware that you don't absorb their anger and take it home to your spouse or your significant relationship. If you regularly hang out with a narcissist, beware that person may drain you because the whole conversation and focus will be about them. It will be about the job they lost or don't have, their sickness and pain, lack of money, and anything that has to do with their needs. You may try to get a couple of words in, but they are good at bringing the focus back to them.

The goal is always to get their needs met. It is nothing more than being the center of attention. Your needs and what you would like to say will not matter. It is all about their self-centeredness. They will make you feel bad if you try to point it out. They are the kings and queens of spinning a story or a conversation. Even if you are in a crisis, the narcissist is not capable of empathizing with you. Remember, most are not capable of showing empathy. They will only drain you like a vampire. I will talk more about that in the next chapter.

Try asking yourself the following questions:

- How do you feel after spending time with the people in your circle?
- Do you feel happy?
- Do you feel refreshed?
- Were you challenged positively?
- Did you feel physically sick or emotionally drained?
- Do you feel depressed or in pain?

Be careful. You may be absorbing others' feelings and pain if you are an empath. You may be entertaining a narcissist. It just may be entertaining someone who has had a bad day. That is okay if their energy is normally positive. Just make sure you are watching the company you keep.

5

ENERGY VAMPIRES AND THEIR VICTIMS

Narcissists, as you are starting the see, can be draining and can suck the life out of a person, like an empath. The narcissistic personality thinks empaths are weak and foolish because they are sensitive and willing to give of themselves, sometimes to a fault. Empaths can be played as a fool until they get tired of being used by the self-absorbed narcissist and others like them. Remember the definition of a narcissist according to Merriam-Webster, an extremely self-centered person who has an exaggerated sense of self-importance

Empaths are highly empathic and sensitive. Unfortunately, some empaths have not learned how to keep their emotions in check. Empaths being highly sensitive by nature does not help.

Narcissists tend not to show emotions or any type of sensitivity because they have none. However, they will take their gift of manipulation and use it to connect with the caring empath. Because empaths can easily put themselves in another's shoes, they become a target for the narcissists' use.

Empaths will take the time to listen and help others in most situations where there is a need. But unfortunately, they are not always aware of when they are being conned and manipulated. Because their empathy is so big, they are just always ready to meet a need.

Since the narcissist is self-absorbed, they will always need someone else to take care of them. They don't have any problem bringing their problems and needs to someone else to take care of. They are too selfish to care about another's situation.

When they start a conversation, it will usually be with the letter "I" as an opening statement. I am so upset. I need to pay my rent. I need to get my car fixed. I need to borrow some money, and I need whatever you want to fill in the blanks. Helping another is out of the question unless there is something in it for the narcissist.

Beware of the narcissist who shows signs of caring or affection. If a narcissist shows up with a gift or offers you something out of the blue, be afraid. They usually want something from you, even if it is you listening to another one of their problems or sad stories.

Christel Broederlow, in her writing "What Is An Empath?" agrees that "Empaths Are Good Listeners" and are very affectionate in personality. She writes,

Empaths are often very affectionate in personality and expression, so they are great listeners and counselors. They will find themselves helping others and often putting their own needs aside to do so. This is why we find so many empaths in careers connected with compassion, such as healers, clergy, counselors, and caregivers.

I'm a social worker and counselor. I have listened to many people and their problems. The ones I find most interesting are those who blame others for their problems. They never seem to take responsibility for the issues they usually create. The men tend to be the most manipulative of narcissists. However, some women come through that are full of themselves as well and can manipulate also.

When treating those with an addiction, addicts can become narcissistic by badly needing to feed their addiction. They become self-absorbed with their addiction. All they think about and will lie about is getting their next high or fix.

They will con, manipulate, and steal without any remorse. Addicts can become draining when they need to get high on a substance or use alcohol. They don't get tired of begging and lying to get their needs to use met.

It amazes me how some narcissists can brag and laugh about how well they have conned and hurt other people, especially when acting in their addiction. Narcissists can share all the negatives things they have done to others, especially those dealing with substances abuse, without a drop of remorse. When you have ever dealt with a narcissist, you may have come to know they are anything but sensitive, compassionate, and caring (again, unless they want something). You can attempt to share a problem with a narcissist after they have drained the life out of you, but it will be to no avail. They will act like they are listening when you are pouring your heart out. However, if it is not about them, they will lose interest in the conversation very quickly.

If you are an emotional empath, you can easily be a target for the narcissist because they are like energy vampires. Narcissists will suck the energy right out of an emotional empath. They can see the emotional empath coming a mile away. I realize even being a counselor, they can see me coming too. However, I try to pay attention to those who start to drain me and take over most of the conversation when in group sessions. Orloff says (p107),

Energy vampires are attracted to the openness and loving hearts of empaths. Sensitive people need to be prepared for them. I've found that some relationships are positive and energizing for my empath patients, but others are draining.

She speaks of developing strategies to deal with them effectively. That way, the narcissist can't take you by surprise. They are truly full of surprises. Think about the times you've been charmed by the narcissist into doing something you told yourself and them you were not going to do but found yourself doing it anyway. They know how to wear a person down because they have studied and figured out if you are sensitive to another's emotions and problems. Here is the self-assessment list Orloff shared in, The Empath's Survival Guide "How do you know if you've met an energy vampire?" (p108),

- You feel tired and want to go to sleep.
- You're suddenly in a terrible mood.
- You feel sick.
- You don't feel seen or heard.
- You reach for sugar or carbohydrates for a boost.
- You start doubting yourself and become self-critical.
- You become anxious, angry, or negative when you didn't feel that way before.
- You feel shamed, controlled, or judged.

If you are an emotional empath, you are a target for the narcissist. Narcissists are good at playing on another's emotions and sympathy. If you have low self-esteem, you will attract the narcissist. They will manipulate and control others by criticizing to get what they want to make themselves feel good, and others feel bad. Be careful how much personal information you give a narcissist. They will use it against you and use it to manipulate you. If you are an emotional empath, the narcissist will eat you alive if you are unaware of their personality disorder. The narcissist is aware of your loving and caring heart. They will suck the life out of you with their grandiose and self-importance act. Orloff says (p109),

> Narcissists act as if the world revolves around them. They have an inflated sense of importance and entitlement. They need to be the center of attention and require endless praise. You must compliment them to get their approval.

How draining is that always having to inflate another's ego to help make them feel good? While at the same time, your emotional needs go unmet. The conversation sharing is never equal. Giving and taking are never equal. They will take and think nothing about giving to others. Unlike empaths who are so empathic to others' needs and willing to put themselves in another's shoes. While the narcissist only sees their shoes needing to be filled.

When you are left feeling drained every time you have a conversation with someone you know or are in a relationship with, you may be dealing with a narcissistic energy vampire. The sense that you are always the one giving in a relationship but never receiving. You may be in a relationship with a narcissist draining you of your giving.

When you are constantly listening to another person's problems without having the opportunity to shares your thoughts and feelings, you are probably dealing with an energy vampire. You are most likely dealing with a narcissist. Maybe it is time to find you a new friend or a new relationship, especially if you feel drained every time or most of the time you interact with the person causing you to feel that way. You do have choices as to how much access people have to you. If it is your spouse, you need to learn how to set healthy boundaries. If you don't know how it may be necessary for your own well-being to get into therapy to get help.

Energy vampires are just what they sound like. They will suck the very life out of you if you let them. So, pay attention to how others make you feel. When you feel drained and crazy most of the time, you may be dealing with an energy vampire or, even worse, a narcissistic energy vampire.

6

DID YOU PICK THE NARCISSIST, OR DID THE NARCISSIST PICK YOU?

I am sorry to say, if you are an emotional empath, you may have been a target of the narcissist. I have had my share of relationships with narcissistic personalities. Every time I thought I was done dealing with a narcissist, another narcissist would befriend me. You may have thought you were done dealing with the narcissists in your life. Just like I thought I was done. The problem is the world is full of narcissists, and the world is also full of empaths.

The empathic personality is always looking for someone to help take care of, and the narcissist is looking for a person to take care of them. Hopefully, I will give you some insight on how narcissistic personalities keep showing up in your life as they have in mine. As I shared in my first book, "Girl, You're Not Crazy. You're dealing with a narcissist" 80% of narcissists are of the male gender, leaving about 20% of narcissists are females. So, you are bound to meet up with a couple of narcissists in your lifetime.

I know they say that opposites attract. For me, I am usually drawn to those who are extroverts - the type of people who are friendly and outgoing. They don't meet any strangers. I am the "come find me" introvert. I get excited when others start the conversation because, by nature, that is not who I am.

I have learned to break the ice because of my profession as a group facilitator and individual counselor. It forces me to speak out. However, I love it when someone comes along and breaks the ice for me. I love when someone leads the conversation, and all I need to do is jump right in.

Narcissists know how to lead the conversation and lead it well. They are usually fishing for sensitive and emotional empaths or people they can use. They are very observant. They are looking for something or someone they can use. They are looking to see who they can con and manipulate. They can tell who seems more compassionate and eager to help. They will present like they have it all together until they have your attention.

Once they know they have another's attention, the games begin. They start to share their needs because they have picked up on who likes helping or taking care of those who are down on their luck.

I have compassion for hurting people. With that comes the homeless, the drug addicts, the alcoholics, and those in broken relationships. I try to be positive and bring positive encouragement to those who need it. I like to encourage broken-hearted and hurting people. I enjoy helping and building up others, but that can turn into rescuing others if I am not careful. I am like a magnet to hurting people. Just like a magnet, I draw some good metals and some bad metals. The energy that I have in me to help others draws people that need my help. That is alright because I still love helping others. However, the same energy also draws people that don't need my help, like the narcissist.

Narcissists are usually drawn to the helper in me. Narcissists, because of their opposite energy, are generally attracted to me like a fix-it magnet. Their self-absorbed energy seems to sniff out empaths. So, I become a target to the narcissist because they always come with a need.

I found it interesting to think back on most of my relationships with narcissists and how they came about. Initially, it seemed like I was heavily pursued because of sincere interest. Now, I feel like I was being targeted. A couple of relationships I found myself in were nothing that I was personally interested in initially. However, I now believe I gave in to some of the relationships thinking that the person's attraction to me was good and sincere, and they truly wanted to connect with me.

Sometimes I thought the narcissistic person wanted to build a life with me, not considering the person saw me as an opportunity to meet their own selfish needs. It became clear when my needs went unmet most of the time. When my needs were not a priority or even considered most of the time, I started to realize the relationship was not about me at all. Sure, in the beginning, there was a lot of effort put into getting my attention. Things were said and done that led me to believe that my wants and needs were as important as those of the narcissists.

However, things always changed once I was committed to the relationship, with the narcissist being the center of attention. It was more like I was being taken for granted. That is a hard pill to swallow being the sensitive, compassionate, and giving person I am. Only to find out I was dealing with a narcissist, the opposite of who I am. I realized I was dealing with a narcissist who was self-centered, arrogant, and self-absorbed.

Empaths usually go all in emotionally, while narcissists are only committed to themselves. Narcissists are not capable of going all in emotionally. Narcissists, in the beginning, are very charming with their promises to give, love unconditionally and be everything in a relationship. It is just not something they can follow through with. Empaths eat that type of communication up while being charmed and baited by the narcissists. Narcissists are good at what they do as an act. Orloff says,

> Narcissists may appear to have much to give-but they don't. The confusing part is that on the surface they can be smart, funny, thoughtful and generous, but they can't maintain that front in intimate relationships.

At first, it was hard to believe that a human could not possess some level of empathy for another's feeling because I am not wired that way. However, it did not take long after I was in a committed relationship to see the narcissist's behavior changes. There was no longer a need to charm and impress me. There was no longer a need to pursue me. The narcissist had hit the bullseye, me. Then the games began when I expressed their lack of empathy and compassion towards my feelings.

To convince me nothing had changed, I would be accused of being too demanding, jealous, or insecure. Does any of that sound familiar? Words like that were used so the narcissistic person could good gaslit me, make me think I was crazy. I was not crazy. The narcissist was just incapable of caring about another and was not willing to reciprocate in the relationship.

Also, the narcissist would criticize to avoid keeping up the act put on in the first place to draw me in. I would soon find out it was all an act for the narcissist to get what was wanted out of the relationship. This happened with female friends as well. Not just in my intimate relationships. The act was to draw me in to satisfy their selfish needs and use my empathic gift to get what they wanted.

It would initially work because of naivety and being a gullible empath. I would fall for the act like many other empaths that are givers, not takers. Empaths that are compassionate and full of empathy, unlike the non-empathetic and unemotional narcissists, usually get the short end of the stick. It wasn't until I was physically and mentally drained of the narcissist or the narcissist was ready to move on to his next victim that I was able to move on. Orloff also says p111),

> Narcissists can make empaths feel physically ill and depressed. They can beat down self-esteem until empaths no longer believe in themselves.

One thing that is for sure, to be fair, once empaths recognize they have a gift as an empath, they must take responsibility to protect their gift. Learning about who you are and your personality type is vital, especially if you find yourself in a relationship with a narcissist.

Empaths also need to learn how to manage their personality type so that they will not be taken advantage of by narcissists and other selfish people. Finally, watch to see if there is reciprocity in the relationship. Is the other person willing to give and take as much as you are?

Empaths must pay attention to how others treat them when they have a need. If a person feels like they are being used, they probably are. If it feels like a one-way accommodation, it probably is one-way and will continue to be if boundaries are not set. Remember, narcissists have an eye for empaths because empaths are gullible and compassionate towards helping others. Narcissists will target empaths and succeed if the empath is not aware of the narcissists' conning and negative behaviors.

Make sure you get to know their history fully. It can be a friendship, courtship, and including a marriage relationship. A narcissist will pick you by targeting you for their own selfish needs to be met and not necessarily because they want to have a committed friendship or relationship.

The following are a few of Judith Orloff's Strategies for protecting yourself from the narcissist (111-112),

- Lower your expectations of the narcissist's emotional capabilities.

- Don't let yourself be manipulated.

- Don't expect a narcissist to respect your sensitivities-they are extremely cold people.

- Don't fall in love with a narcissist. Run in the opposite direction no matter how attracted you feel.

- Try to avoid working with a narcissistic boss-but if you can't leave, don't let your self-esteem depend on your boss's reactions.

To learn more strategies for protecting yourself from the narcissist, check out Judith Orloff's book "The Empath's Survival Guide, Life Strategies for Sensitive People."

7

NO THANKS, I WILL DRIVE

As I have mentioned, I am an introverted empath. That means I am more comfortable at home, in small groups of people, and I avoid loud spaces and noises if possible.

The only place I have become comfortable with loud noise is at church. I love worship music. Most worship music brings me joy and peace. While most empaths are introverted, some are extroverted as well. Some empaths are a combination of both introverts and extroverts. I am with Orloff when she says,

> Introverted empaths, like me, have a minimal tolerance for socialization and

small talk. They tend to be quieter at gatherings and prefer leaving early. Often they arrive in their own cars so they don't have to feel trapped or dependent on others for a ride.

You don't know how freeing that felt when I read that paragraph in Orloff's book. I hate riding with other people to social events or gatherings, especially with extrovert-type personalities. That does not mean I hate extroverted people because I am attracted to the opposite of myself when it comes to relationships. I just know after being in an atmosphere with a lot of people and a lot of noise, I become physically and emotionally drained for a long time.

Being around family is not so draining because they know me and will not be offended if I get quiet or if I am the first to leave a party. I think they may be used to that. I only have a few close friends, and I usually meet with them one-on-one or in a church fellowship-type setting where all the attention is not on me. I am not the one having to present or hold down the conversation. However, I sometimes do.

Whenever I socialize, I prefer to drive myself. That way, when I feel tired or overwhelmed by a crowd or too much energy, I can leave. As an introverted empath, there is nothing worse for me than being stuck at a place that I am ready to exit but can't leave. My mood may change the longer I am exposed to too much energy. I wouldn't want to offend anyone by shutting down. Therefore, when I am asked if I want to ride with someone else, unless that person is like me or I trust them to take me home when I am ready, it will be a, No thanks! I will drive myself.

If it happens to be a narcissist offering to drive, I know I best be ready to stay if they want to stay, especially if it is an extroverted narcissist. The narcissist is going to want to leave when they are ready to leave, extroverted or not. You may see them throw a tantrum if they are asked to leave early.

Narcissists are going to meet their needs first. If they want to hang out, it will not matter how late or how long. If the narcissist is driving, they will either stay or leave with an attitude because they did not get their way. If you are an empath who is ready to leave, not only will you be drained because you are ready to leave, but now you are stuck dealing with the emotional drama of dealing with a narcissist. Remember, empaths absorb others' emotions and energy. We can be easily stimulated by too much excitement, noise, or someone else frustration. No thanks, I will drive.

8

TAKING CARE OF YOUR PHYSICAL AND EMOTIONAL HEALTH

There was a time I did not know how to say no. I said yes to everything. I would do things I did not want to do or feel like doing because I would feel guilty if I said no. I would go places or do something with others I did not want to do.

I would take phone calls in the middle of the night for problems that could not be solved even if I tried. That did not stop the phone from ringing at night. I learned to be careful when telling certain people, especially a narcissist, "call me anytime." Some people with non-emergencies would do just that, call me anytime.

Allowing people with non-emergencies or problems I could do nothing about would just cause me emotional stress and a lack of sleep. That was not taking care of myself by allowing things like that to interfere with my rest. I finally learned that if I did not take care of myself as an empath, I would be burnt out most of the time. If I am fixing problems all day at work as a social worker and all night, that is not healthy.

In taking care of myself, I started setting healthy boundaries when it came to how late I would be accepting phone calls at night. If someone made a pattern of calling me with non-emergency phone calls at night, I just would not answer the phone. I love caller ID.

My father had a saying, "I can show you better than I can tell you." So, when I stopped answering my phone late at night for non-emergency calls, things got better for me.

In the beginning, it was hard being a sensitive empath not jumping up to answer the phone, afraid I would miss rescuing the person on the other end of the line. However, the older I've got, the easier it has become. Those days of staying up half the night listening to the same person's problems they were unwilling to do anything about got old quickly.

Don't get me wrong, if someone calls me in the middle of the night with a real emergency, I am up and listening. However, some people will call because they believe I will answer the phone and know I will listen anytime.

I am all about helping others who genuinely have a problem and who I genuinely can help. However, I am more about my self-care first now that I am older and wiser. That means getting my sleep so I can wake up feeling fresh the next morning and not feeling drained from listening to someone else's drama.

There is a difference between caring for someone in a real crisis versus drama. I try hard to avoid drama people and their drama conversations. That's how I take care of myself, and if you are smart, you will take care of yourself too.

Just in case you didn't know this, it is not selfish to take care of yourself. We are, in fact, responsible for taking care of our self-care first.

Most have heard the airline steward announcing in the event of an emergency, "Put Your Mask on First." You can't help someone if you are not safe and secure. If we are not physically and emotionally healthy, how should we expect to help someone else?

It is alright to protect yourself from those who try to take advantage of your gift as the compassionate and sensitive empath. Likewise, it is okay to protect yourself from those who would try to use your gift to manipulate you for their own personal gain emotionally.

Narcissists are very good at taking advantage of others for their own needs to be met. Remember, narcissists have a sense of entitlement. They expect preferential treatment from others. They love when others cater to their needs without considering the other person's needs.

If you are an emotional empath, it will be important to protect yourself physically and emotionally from the narcissist. A narcissist will not be quick to care for you if you are sick and need their help. However, a narcissist will not have a problem with waking you up in the middle of the night with some foolishness. A narcissist will ask you to get out of your sickbed to do them a favor because they are self-centered. They will want you to cook, clean, and always feel their problem is more important than yours.

If you allow a narcissist to tap into your sensitive and compassionate emotions, you will find yourself stopping your own care to help the narcissist. That same narcissist would not do the same for you. Try

YOU'RE STILL NOT CRAZY   71

getting sick after you have been assisting a narcissist. You may get their attention for a few minutes, but don't be sick for too long.

Narcissists are not capable of being sensitive or empathic to others' needs. Therefore, they may try to act concerned if you need them, but an act can only last so long. So soon as a more comfortable opportunity comes along for the narcissist, they are subject to make an excuse to bolt on you.

You can beg most narcissists to stick around when you are in a crisis. Still, they just are not capable of feeling the same amount of sensitivity as the empath. If you happen to be in a love relationship with a narcissist, you may have difficulty setting boundaries. They are so charming and captivating when it comes to getting what they want. It is usually after the narcissist have been very cold and mean that empaths start to get the picture they are dealing with an unaffectionate self-absorbed narcissist. After experiencing multiple situations of emotional abuse, an empath may muster up enough strength to move on if necessary. To protect yourself from the narcissist, here are a few things Orloff writes (p.111-112),

- Lower your expectations of the narcissist's emotional capabilities.

- Don't let yourself be manipulated.

- Don't' expect a narcissist to respect your sensitivities-they are extremely cold people.

- Don't fall in love with a narcissistic. Run in the opposite direction no matter how attracted you feel.

- Try to avoid working with a narcissistic boss-but if you can't leave, don't let your self-esteem depend on your boss's reactions.

Avoiding being in a serious relationship with a narcissist may be the only way to avoid being a victim of their selfish and manipulative behaviors. It is hard to avoid someone if you are married to, living with, or working for them. However, being aware of the characteristics of a narcissist may help with knowing how to interact when you have an encounter with their craziness. Narcissists can be drama kings or queens. I will talk about this in the next chapter.

9

PROTECTING YOURSELF FROM DRAMA QUEENS AND KINGS

Narcissists tend to be drama queens and kings. Most of us will have a friend, or family member, who is a drama addict. They don't feel right when things are calm and peaceful.

A drama queen or king thrives on drama. It is easy to avoid the drama of those who are not close to you and are narcissists. However, once you get caught up in an intimate relationship with a narcissist, it can be hard for an empath to get out because of the emotional attachment.

What are empaths?

Empaths are sensitive and emotional personalities. Sometimes empaths can be driven by their sensitivities and emotions. Narcissists are good at playing on others' emotions. Narcissists can be fast talkers and good actors. When they come with their drama, it can be made for the movies or live television. They are so well-rehearsed with exaggerations of their dramatic stories they can be believable. When they want something, narcissists can make up a convincing story that you would never think could be a lie or something that never happened. I have seen narcissists come to tears on a story that just was not true. They will lie or exaggerate about being sick; they will lie to convince you that you said something you never said, and they will swear on their mother's grave about the lie. All a narcissist is interested in is getting what they want or need. They will drain you with their drama to get what they want if you allow them to. Have you ever seen anyone who always got a sad story to tell or a horrible situation they can't wait to share?

They never come with good news. It is always something depressing and real intense. The atmosphere can be peaceful and full of joy until that type of drama queen or king shows up. If you

YOU'RE STILL NOT CRAZY   75

are an emotional empath, you can become an emotional wreck dealing with a narcissistic drama king or queen. Orloff on the Drama Queen or Kings says (p118),

> These types drain sensitive people by overloading them with nonstop dramas. These dramas impose too much information and stimulation for empaths to process. Their histrionics deplete us.

Before giving a narcissist your ear, heart, and emotions, you might want to think about who and what you are dealing with. Some of you may already be involved in a significant relationship or friendship relationship with a drama queen or king narcissist. If you happen to find yourself in a relationship with a drama queen or king, here are a few protection strategies Orloff suggest (p. 119),

> - Don't ask these people how they are doing. You don't want to know
>
> - Breathe deeply. When drama queens or kings start up, breathe deeply, stay calm, and do not get caught up in their story.

- Set kind but firm limits. For example, you might say to a friend who keeps cancelling plans, "I'm sorry for all your mishaps, but let's not reschedule until things settle down for you and you can show up." Setting limits helps you communicate clearly and doesn't reinforce their behavior.

Asking a drama queen or king how they are doing is like opening a can of snakes, not just worms. By the time they are through, you could end up drained or traumatized. At worst, you may think you are crazy after the drama queen or king convinces you are something you know is not true.

When you finally figure things out, you may become frustrated for allowing the narcissist or drama queens and kings to draw you in. Both can be fast talkers, charmers and know how to captivate your attention. On the other hand, an empath would need to take deep breaths to release intense emotions and anxiety from too much information.

Knowing your limits will help you to stop the drama queen or king before they draw you in. Remember, it is alright to take care of yourself. You can say no, and it is okay to set kind but firm limits. If you don't learn to take care of yourself as an empath, people will take advantage of your gift. People will drain the life out of you and make you think you are crazy in the process. However, you are not crazy. You are probably a sensitive and emotional empath dealing with a narcissist.

10

YOU'RE NOT CRAZY

I know you can feel like you are crazy when you find yourself in and out of relationships with narcissists. You're not crazy. It is possible because you are a sensitive and emotional empath; you care deeply for others.

You're not crazy; you're probably a kind, loving person that loves helping others. When you love people and happen to be an emotional empath, you can easily absorb their feelings and problems. Unfortunately, because we all deal with people at some point in our life, we are bound to experience a relationship with a narcissist.

You may have a narcissistic spouse, parent, child, or friend. Your boss or co-worker may be a narcissist.

It is hard to avoid every narcissist in the world. Remember, the world is full of them, both male and female. Unfortunately, it was destined to happen in these last days that we are living in.

People care more about getting what they want than how they may be hurting others to get it. The love of money has driven people to lie and scheme as it has never been before. We hear on the news all the time how wealthy people have broken the law to get more money, get their children in the best schools, and tax frauds to avoid spending their money. We hear about the Politian's and what they do to get in office.

Those situations are public information, but we don't hear how our own family, friends, and those in our close relationships con and manipulate us. We don't hear how our bosses and co-workers flaunt their feelings and entitlements in our faces and take advantage of people on their jobs. This happens because people are lovers of themselves, arrogant, greedy, and lovers of money. It is the last day prophecy being fulfilled according to the scripture I mentioned earlier found in 2 Timothy 3:1-3 (AMP),

> *But understand this, that in the last days dangerous times [of great*

stress and trouble] will come [difficult days that will be hard to bear]. 2 For people will be lovers of self [narcissistic, self-focused], lovers of money [impelled by greed], boastful, arrogant, revilers, disobedient to parents, ungrateful, unholy and profane.

These are dangerous times we are living in. I have never heard of so much crime before in my lifetime.

There are neighborhood shootings, police officer-involved shootings, and carjacking's happening all over the city. Nowhere seems to be safe. Just the things happening in the world alone are enough to make people feel crazy. If you are an empath, you are subject to emotionally absorb the problems and suffering the world is experiencing daily.

It is the year 2021. We have been experiencing the effects of the COVID-19 pandemic for over a year now. People are still feeling isolated and overwhelmed. They need each other. People need to check in with one another. People need to reach out to one another if they are having a hard time.

Mental Health crisis centers are being advertised as a common trend these days. Mental health treatment and counselors are much needed today. People who are suffering from depression and other mental health problems need to ask for help. They are not crazy. They are people who need help with balancing their mood when it has become too low for a long period of time. However, those who love drama, like I talked about in the last chapter, will drain you if you are an emotional empath.

Suppose you try to fix everyone's problems, especially the narcissists you were never created to do. In that case, you will feel crazy or go crazy trying to. Don't try to. Just focus on what you can handle and leave the rest to the God of the universe. He can handle it more than you ever will.

The narcissist will not mind dumping all their problems on others. Don't allow the narcissist or other drama queens or kings to manipulate you or call you crazy when you don't go along with their games and craziness. You were given a gift to help others but not to be used or abuse by others. Give those people over to God in prayer. He is called God for a reason.

Learn how to listen, pray, and balance yourself when it comes to helping others. Try not to let other's put more on you than you can bear, especially when God almighty doesn't allow them to do so. When you feel yourself becoming depressed or overwhelmed listening and helping others, it is time to take a break. Just breathe. Stop thinking you are crazy for being who you are if you are a sensitive and compassionate empath. You don't have to feel guilty when you choose not to help. You may be dealing with a self-absorb unemotional narcissist who does not mind making you feel crazy.

REFERENCES

Definition Empathy,
https://www.merriamwebster.com/dictionary/empathy

Definition Empath,
https://www.merriam-webster.com/dictionary/empath

Definition Narcissist,
https://www.merriam-webster.com/dictionary/narcissist

Definition Narcissism
https://www.merriam-webster.com/dictionary/narcissism

Hypochondriac
https://www.merriam-webster.com/dictionary/hypochondriac

Preston Ni, M.S.B.A., Psychology Today, Posted 9/14/2014,
10 Signs That You're in a Relationship with a Narcissist
https://www.psychologytoday.com/us/blog/communication-success/201409/10-signs-youre-in-relationship-narcissist

Judith Orloff, MD (Feb 19, 2010). Traits Empathic People Share and how to look out for yourself if you are one. Psychology Today

Judith Orloff, MD (2017, 2018). The Empath's Survival Guide: Life Strategies for Sensitive People. Sounds True Boulder, Co

Definition egocentrism,
https://www.merriam-webster.com/dictionary/egocentrism

Broederlow, Christel. (2020, Feb 11). What is an Empath? https://www.learnreligions.com/traits-of-empaths-1724671

Updated on Apr 07, 2020, Jodi Clarke, Cognitive vs. Emotional Empathy. https://www.verywellmind.com/cognitive-and-emotional-empathy-4582389

ABOUT THE AUTHOR

Carolyn Booker Pierce is a licensed social worker, teacher, mentor, and spiritual leader born and raised in Columbus, Ohio.

After leaving a career of almost 20 years in accounts payable and claims auditing, Carolyn followed her passion in the area of social services. She then graduated with a BA at Capital University to become a licensed social worker. Carolyn gravitates to chemical dependency counseling as a substance abuse group and individual counselor.

Later she took her years of experience as a substance abuse counselor into her local county jail to serve inmates struggling with substance abuse, alcoholism, and family relationship problems. She is known for listening to others without judgment as they process their everyday life problems.

Carolyn desires to help people grow, heal from their past, and move on to a healthy future. She enjoys spending time with her family, church worship center, traveling, writing, and empowering others.

facebook.com/carolyn.pierce.5245

ALSO BY CAROLYN BOOKER-PIERCE

Because the Lord is My Shepherd: Psalm 23 and Me

Girl, You're Not Crazy. You're Dealing With a Narcissist

Loving the Addict: While Taking Care of Yourself First

Abortion!: George and Giovanna

More Than A Village: Raising Black Men in America

www.ingramcontent.com/pod-product-compliance
Lightning Source LLC
Chambersburg PA
CBHW071504070526
44578CB00001B/433